The
Voice

Story and pictures by

R.W. Metlen

Paulist Press
New York, Mahwah, N.J.

Text and cover design by Saija Autrand, Faces Type & Design

Library of Congress Control Number: 2016956575

ISBN: 978-0-8091-5353-4

Published by Paulist Press
997 Macarthur Boulevard
Mahwah, New Jersey 07430 USA

www.paulistpress.com

Printed and bound in the
United States of America

"Whoever finds his life will lose it, and whoever loses his life for my sake will find it."

Matthew 10:39

For Kit and Meryl

"Follow me,"

said the Voice.

"Follow me,"

said the Voice.

I did not want to listen.

"I love you," said the Voice.

The Voice, whoever it was, was very intrusive.

"Go away. I'm fishing."

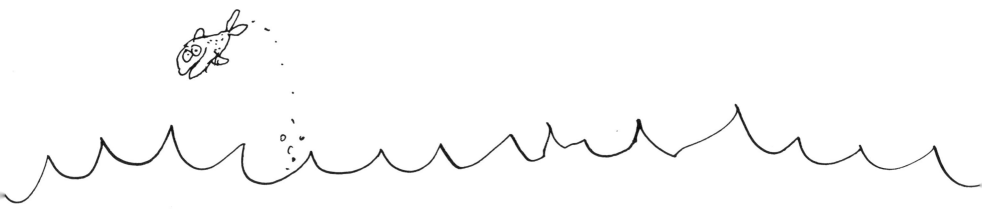

I could feel it watching me.

Eventually, I caught a fish.
I was feeling very proud of myself.

"You're welcome," said the Voice.

The Voice was silent, but it didn't go away.

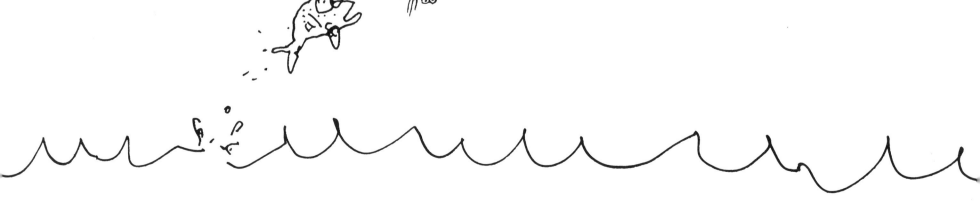

I lay back to take a nap.

Then, quite unexpectedly, my boat sprung a leak.

Sploosh

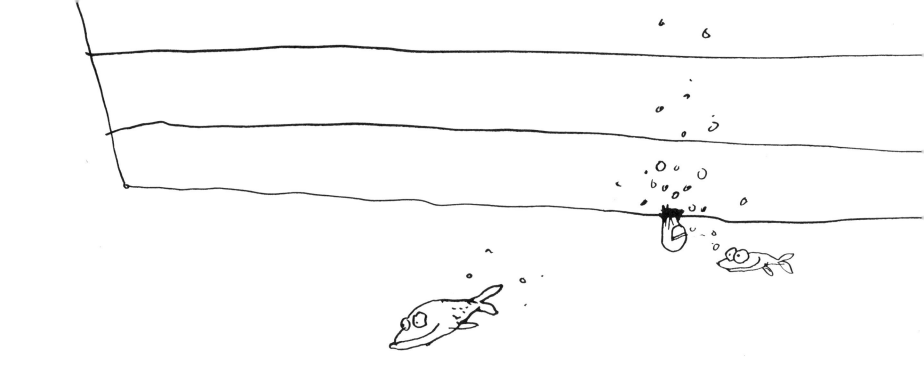

I found the hole and plugged it
with one of my toes.

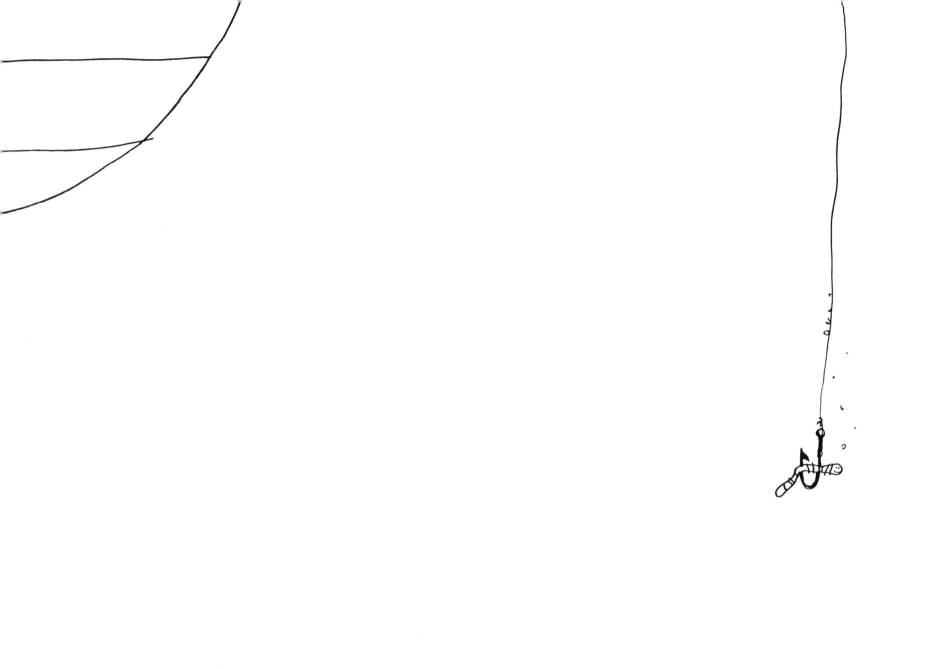

That Voice was putting holes

in my boat!

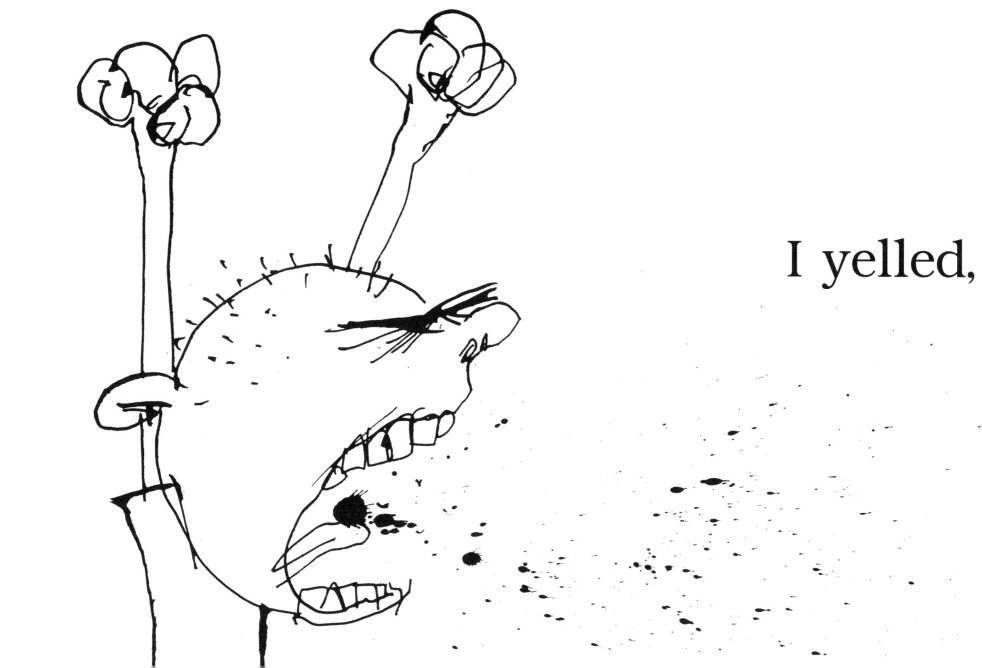

I yelled,

"VOICE, I DO NOT APPRECIATE YOU!"

"Stop behaving so badly," said the Voice,

"and just follow me."

The Voice let out a long sigh.

My boat began to leak again.

At first, I refused to plug the hole.

I thought, "I'll show that Voice how tough I am.
I'll just go ahead and drown."

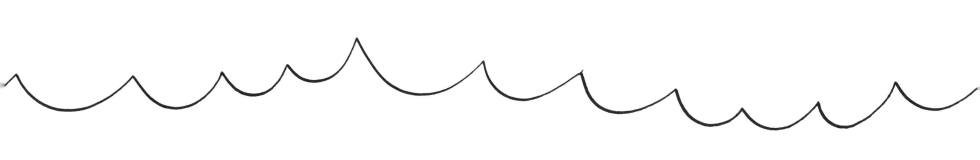

Then I got scared.

I didn't really want to drown.

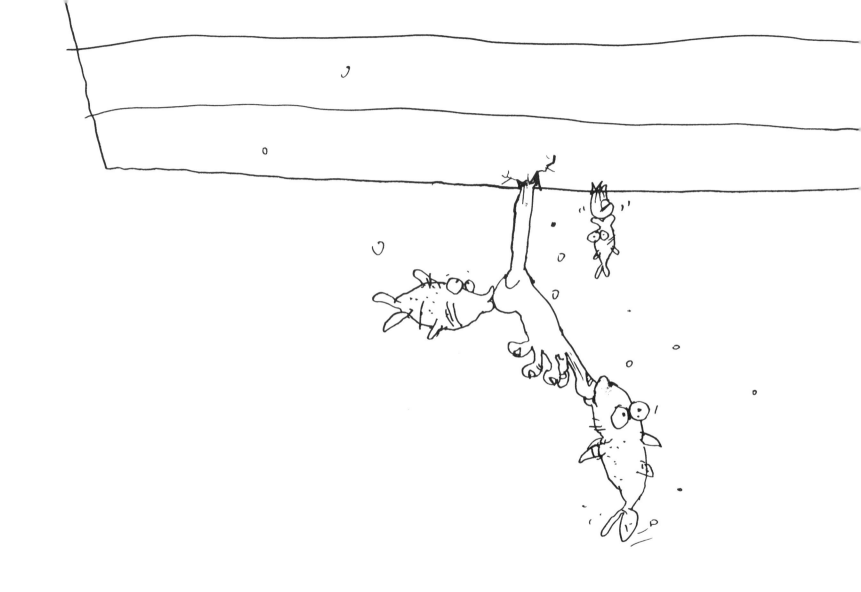

It took my whole leg to plug that hole. I could feel the

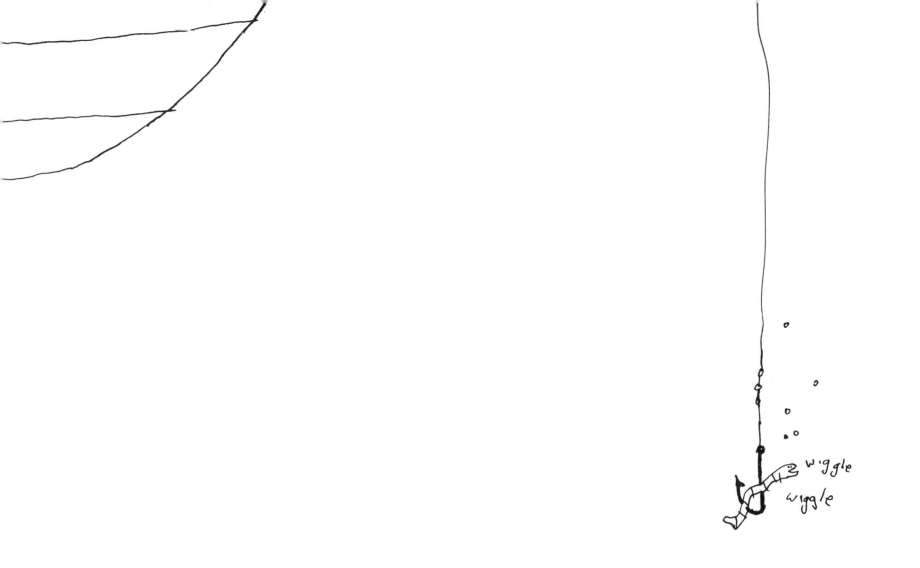

wiggle

wiggle

fish tickling my foot in the water below.

"Stupid fish," I thought.

Everybody was picking on me.

I wanted to go home, but I couldn't reach my oars.

I was stuck!

I began to cry.

"Follow me," said the Voice.

"Why won't you leave me alone?" I asked.
I was feeling very sorry for myself.

"I already told you. I love you," said the Voice.

"Follow me."

"I CAN'T! If I move, my boat will sink!"

"Let it sink," said the Voice.

"LET IT SINK?" I asked.

"Don't you care about me?

I'll drown! I'll become fish food! I can't swim!"

"You won't have to swim.

Just follow me,"

said the Voice.

I sat there, wondering what to do.

This seemed like an awfully dirty trick.

How did I know I could trust the Voice?

There seemed to be no other option.

So I pulled my toe out of the first hole.
Immediately water began filling the boat.

"Better pull your other leg out too,"
 recommended the Voice,
"or the boat will drag you down with it."

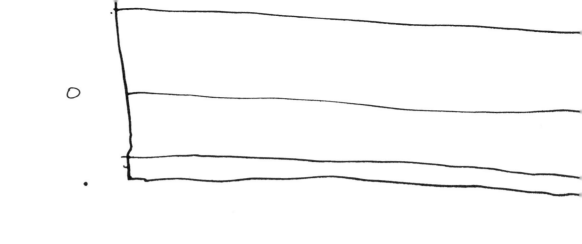

So I did.

The cold water rushed in as the boat sank.

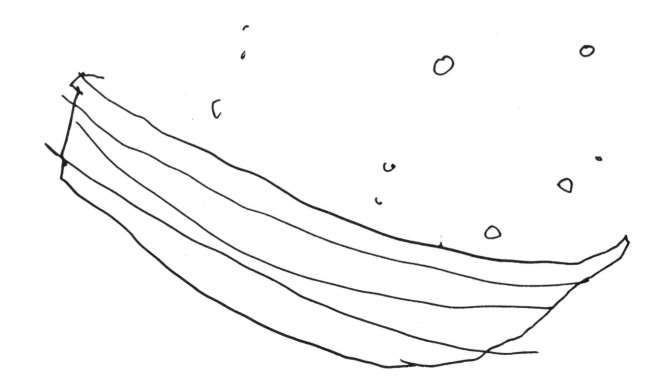

I called out,
  "Help! Voice!
    Help me!"

"Open your eyes," said the Voice.

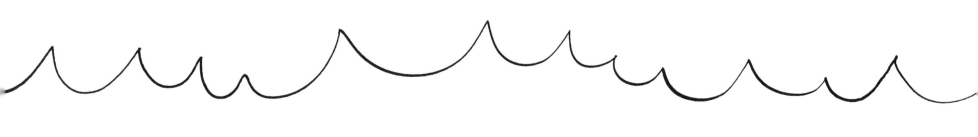

"Follow me,"

said the Voice.

So I did.